A Whole Lot of
Spin & Zip

A Whole Lot of Spin & Zip

101 Quotes on Speed & Action

Jim Walker

Writers Club Press

San Jose   New York   Lincoln   Shanghai

A Whole Lot of Spin & Zip
101 Quotes on Speed & Action

Writers Club Press
an imprint of iUniverse, Inc.

For information address:
iUniverse, Inc.
5220 S. 16th St., Suite 200
Lincoln, NE 68512
www.iuniverse.com

ISBN: 0-595-21044-9

Printed in the United States of America

For

Patti, Kathryn, Ben,
John, Matthew

&

Bob Cooper

&

The Visible Human Team

Preface

Thousands of years ago in the book of Proverbs, King Solomon wrote that a word fitly spoken is like apples of gold in a setting of silver. Now, as then, a timely quote can indeed be a great and incredible treasure.

Many of these quotes come from my favorite authors, while others were found on Internet sites, in e-mails from friends and colleagues, and even on the back of tea boxes.

I hope that you find some golden favorites here that will stir you to action, move you to courage, and help lead you to realizing your dreams.

Enjoy!

The man who
removes a mountain
begins by carrying away
small stones.

Chinese proverb

In skating over thin ice
our safety
is in our speed.

Ralph Waldo Emerson

Just don't give up trying
to do what you
really want to do…
Where there's
love and inspiration,
I don't think you can
go wrong.

Ella Fitzgerald

Never confuse motion
with action.

Benjamin Franklin

Action, to be productive,
has need of contemplation.
The latter, when it gets to a certain degree of
intensity,
diffuses some of its excess
on the first.
By contemplation the soul draws directly from
the heart of God
the graces which the active life must distribute.

Mother Teresa

Fast and good
is better than
slow and perfect.

Bob Davis
founder of Lycos

Not snow, no, nor rain, nor heat, nor night
keeps them from accomplishing their
appointed courses
with all speed.

Herodotus
(485 BC–425 BC)

The Possible's slow fuse is lit
by the Imagination.

Emily Dickinson

We live
in a moment of history
where change
is so speeded up
that we begin to see
the present
only when it is already disappearing.

R. D. Laing
The Politics of Experience

Wisdom
is better than jewels,
and all that you may desire
cannot compare with her.

Proverbs 8:11

Making art
begins with making hay
while the sun shines.
It begins with getting into the *now* and enjoying
your day.
It begins with giving yourself some small treats
and breaks.
"This is extravagant
but so is God"
is a good attitude to take when treating your
artist to small bribes and beauties.
Because remember,
you are the cheapskate,
not God.

Julia Cameron
The Artist's Way

The less effort,
the faster and more powerful
you will be.

Bruce Lee

While we are postponing,
life speeds by.

Seneca
(3 BC–65 AD)

It is impossible to travel faster
than the speed of light,
and certainly not desirable,
as one's hat
keeps blowing off.

Woody Allen

The backbone of surprise
is fusing
speed with secrecy.

Karl von Clausewitz

Love is swift of foot;
Love's a man of war,
And can shoot,
And can hit from far.

George Herbert

Great things
are not done by impulse,
but by a series of small things brought together.

Vincent Van Gogh

I have not failed.
I've just found 10,000 ways
that won't work.

Thomas Edison

There is more to life
than increasing its speed.

Mohandas Gandhi

Only those who
take leisurely what
the people of the world
are busy about
can be busy about what
the people of the world
take leisurely.

Taoist Maxim

Have you ever noticed?
Anybody
going slower than you
is an idiot,
and anyone
going faster than you
is a maniac.

George Carlin

A computer lets you make more mistakes faster
than any invention
in human history–
with the possible exceptions
of handguns and tequila.

Mitch Ratcliffe

Make haste slowly.

Abraham Lincoln

If I live with the anxiety
to go fast,
I will not live well.
My addiction to speed
will make me sick.
The art of living
is about learning how to
give time
to each and every thing.

Carlo Petrini
founder of Slow Food

When you look at someone who's moving fast,
the thing that's being expressed is
movement–which is effortless.
The guys who are tense,
the guys who are straining,
have lost the race.
The race goes to the athlete
who's in control–
of his body,
of his breathing,
of his rhythm.

John Smith
Olympic sprint coach

Every beetle is a gazelle
in the eyes of its mother.

Moorish Proverb

There is only one time
that is important–NOW!
It is the most important time because it is the
only time that
we have any power.

Leo Tolstoy

Action this day!

Winston Churchill

In democratic centuries
when almost everyone
is engaged in active life,
the darting speed of a quick,
superficial mind
is at a premium,
while slow, deep thought
is excessively undervalued.

Alexis de Toqueville
Democracy in America

The ancestor of every action
is a thought.

Ralph Waldo Emerson

The power in a karate punch comes from
speed,
not muscle;
it comes from
a focused "pop"
at the end of the whip. That's why petite people
can learn to break boards with their hands:
it doesn't take
calluses or brute strength,
just the ability to generate a focused thrust with
speed.

David Allen
Getting Things Done

You learn how to
cut down trees
cutting them down.

Bateke proverb

Fanaticism consists of
redoubling your efforts
when you have
forgotten your aim.

George Santayana

The wise do sooner
what fools do later.
Both do the same;
all that differs is the *when*...
There is only one good way to see the light:
as soon as possible.
Otherwise,
you do out of necessity
what you might have done
with pleasure.

Baltasar Gracian
The Art of Worldly Wisdom

Luke looks uncertainly out at the ship.
Luke
Master, moving stones around is one thing.
This is totally different.

Yoda
No! No different! Only different in your mind.
You must unlearn what you have learned.

Luke
(focusing quietly)
All right, I'll give it a try.

Yoda
No! Try not.
Do. Or do not.
There is no try.

It is always with
the best intentions
that the worst work is done.

Oscar Wilde

When a Southwest plane pulls into the gate,
employees in ground operations run for the air-
craft like a pit crew scrambling to get an Indy
car back on the track ...
It's not unusual to see flight attendants and
pilots working with the provisioning and ramp
people to stock airplanes, pick up trash, and
load bags. Employees have the flexibility and
the willingness to step outside previously
defined job categories and do whatever it takes
to get a flight out on time.

Kevin & Jackie Frieberg
Nuts!

I was too slow a mover.
It was much easier
to be a poet.

T.S. Elliot
*on giving up boxing
in college*

We all know people who are going to…. start a
business…
write a book…
learn to skydive…
build a house…as soon as they "find the time."
BULLSHIT!
When you CARE you MAKE the time… and if
that means saying "NO!" to your friends, your
spouse, your kids (hey, I never said there would
be no sacrifices),
well, there it is!

Tom Peters
*The Professional
Service Firm 50*

If you chase two rabbits,
you will not catch
either one.

Russian Proverb

If you train hard,
you'll not only be hard,
you'll be hard to beat.

Hershel Walker

You can't hit a home run
unless you step up to the plate. You can't catch
fish unless you put your line in the water.
You can't make
your idea a reality
unless you take a whack at it.
Many of our personal goals are stranded on a
little island called "Someday I'll."
Don't wait
for your idea to happen.
Make it happen.

Roger von Oech
*A Whack on the
Side of the Head*

He who would leap far
must first take a long run.

Danish Proverb

All happiness
depends on
a leisurely breakfast.

John Gunther

He only is rich
who owns the day.
There is no king, rich man,
fairy or demon
who possesses
such power as that.

Ralph Waldo Emerson

My greatest point
is my persistence.
I never give up in a match.
However down I am,
I fight until the last ball.
My list of matches shows
that I have turned
a great many so-called
irretrievable defeats
into victories.

Bjorn Borg

No one should imitate the manner of another,
for he would then deserve to be called a grand-
son of nature, not her son.
Given the abundance
of natural forms,
it is important to
go straight to nature.

Leonardo da Vinci

The important thing
in a military operation
is victory,
not persistence.

Sun Tzu
The Art of War

An inventor is simply a person who doesn't take
his education
too seriously.
You see, from the time a person is six years old
until he graduates from college he has to take
three or four examinations a year.
If he flunks once, he is out.
But an inventor is
almost always failing.
He tries and fails maybe
a thousand times.
If he succeeds once
then he's in.
These two things
are diametrically opposite.

Charles Kettering
Engineer & Inventor
General Motors

When we read too fast
or too slowly,
we understand nothing.

Blaise Pascal

The main thing is to keep
the main thing
the main thing.

Stephen Covey
First Things First

We who lived in concentration camps can remember the men who walked through the huts comforting others, giving away their last piece of bread.
They may have been few in number, but they offer sufficient proof that everything can be taken from a man but one thing: the last of the human freedoms–
to choose one's attitude
in any given set of circumstances,
to choose one's own way.

Vicktor Frankl

The secret of success is to
get up early,
work late
and strike oil.

J. D. Rockefeller

If you do not seal the holes,
you will have to
rebuild the walls.

Swahili proverb

You can lead
a horse to water–
but you can't teach it to fish.

Fred Shero
Coach
1975 Stanley Cup Champion
Philadelphia Flyers

If there is no wind, row.

Latin proverb

The present contains
all that there is.
It is holy ground;
for it is the past,
and it is the future.
At the same time it must be observed that an
age is no less past if it existed
two hundred years ago
than if it existed
two thousand years ago.

Alfred North Whitehead
Aims of Education

"Do" is the critical word.

Peter Drucker

There are costs and risks
to a program of action,
but they are far less
than the long-range costs and risks
of a comfortable
program of inaction.

John F. Kennedy

Until the snake is dead,
do not drop the stick.

Ivorian proverb

Collaboration is anything
but an assembly-line process.
It can't be routine and predictable. People col-
laborate precisely because they don't know how
to–or can't–deal effectively with the challenges
they face as individuals. There's uncertainty
because they genuinely don't know how they
will get from here to there.
In that respect, collaboration becomes a neces-
sary technique
to master the unknown.

Michael Schrage
No More Teams

Love, all alike,
no season knows nor clime,
Nor hours, days, months,
which are the rags of time.

John Donne

A quarter of an hour
is worth more
than a thousand gold coins.

Chinese proverb

Avoid the activity trap.
Manage choices
out of your life, not into it.
In the storm of information washing over you,
realize that only a
tiny fraction of it is germane
to your own goals and that
it is that tiny fraction
on which you absolutely have to concentrate.

Take a nap, catch an afternoon matinee.
Conserve energy and you'll have more of it for
the things that really matter.

Watts Wacker
The 500 Year Delta

When a lion roars,
he does not catch game.

Acholi proverb

I consider my ability to arouse enthusiasm
among my people the greatest asset I possess,
and the way to develop the best
that is in a person
is by appreciation
and
encouragement.

Charles Schwab
President, US Steel

A single conversation
with a wise man
is better than
ten years of study.

Chinese Proverb

Always leave enough time in your life to do something that makes you happy, satisfied, even joyous.
That has more of an effect on economic well-being than
any other single factor.

Paul Hawken

I wasted time,
and now
doth time waste me.

William Shakespeare

Go confidently in the direction
of your dreams!
Live the life
you've imagined.
As you simplify your life,
the laws of the universe
will be simpler.

Henry David Thoreau

Never look down
to test the ground
before taking your next step:
only he who keeps
his eye fixed
on the far horizon
will find his right road.

Dag Hammarskjold
Markings

The worst misconception about exemplary performers is that they work harder, know more,
and are more highly motivated than others.
These things sometimes
may be true.
But in years of observing exemplary performers
I have discovered the opposite is generally true:

Exemplary performers
do things more easily
than others do them.

Thomas Gilbert
Human Competence

Our little Spaceship Earth
is right now travelling at
sixty thousand miles an hour around the sun
and is also spinning axially, which, at the lati-
tude of Washington, D. C., adds approximately
one thousand miles per hour to our motion.
Each minute we both spin at one hundred miles
and zip in orbit at one thousand miles.
That is a whole lot of
spin and zip.

Buckminster Fuller
Operating Manual for
Spaceship Earth

In the long run men hit
only what they aim at.
Therefore, though they
should fail immediately,
they had better
aim at something high.

Henry David Thoreau

I care not what your profession or occupation
in life may be;
I care not whether you are a lawyer, a doctor, a
housekeeper, teacher or whatever else,
the principle
is precisely the same.
We must know what
the world needs first
and then invest ourselves
to supply that need,
and success is almost certain.

Russell Conwell
Acres of Diamonds

We are
what we repeatedly do.
Excellence, therefore,
is not an act
but a habit.

Aristotle

Nurture your mind
with great thoughts,
for you will
never go any higher
than you think.

Benjamin Disraeli

I believe that man's greatest hour, in fact, his
greatest fulfillment,
is that moment when he has worked his heart
out for a good cause and lies exhausted
but victorious
on the field of battle,
wherever that field may be.

Vince Lombardi

The victories of good warriors
are not noted
for cleverness or bravery.
Therefore their victories in battle are not flukes.
Their victories are not flukes because they posi-
tion themselves where the will surely win,
prevailing over those who
have already lost.

Sun Tzu
The Art of War

Since the end of World War ll,
the world has been
split between
capitalist and communist,
North and South.
Today, as these old divisions
fade in significance,
a new one arises.
For from now on the world
will be split between the
fast and the slow.

Alvin Toffler
PowerShift

Faster! Faster!
Until the thrill of speed
overcomes the fear of death.

Hunter S. Thompson

You can gain strength, courage and confidence
by every experience in which you really stop
to look fear in the face...
You must do the thing which
you think you cannot do.

Eleanor Roosevelt

The beginning
is the half
of every action.

Greek Proverb

Nothing in the world can take the place of
persistence.
Talent will not;
nothing is more common than unsuccessful
men with talent.
Genius will not;
unrewarded genius
is almost a proverb.
Education will not; the world is full of educated
derelicts.
Persistence and determination alone
are omnipotent.
The slogan 'Press On'
has solved and always
will solve the problems
of the human race.

Calvin Coolidge

There are many willing people
in the world,
some willing to work,
the others
willing to let them.

Robert Frost

You will do foolish things,
but do them
with enthusiasm.

Colette

Whatever you can do
or dream you can,
begin it.
Boldness has genius,
power and magic in it.
Begin it now.

Goethe

Do not fear mistakes—
there are none.

Miles Davis

As the exponential growth of technology continues to accelerate into the first half of the twenty-first century, it will appear to explode into infinity, at least from the limited and linear perspective of contemporary humans.
The progress will ultimately become so fast that it will rupture our ability to follow it.
It will literally get out of our control. The illusion that we have our hand "on the plug," will be dispelled.

Raymond Kurzweil
The Singularity is Near

I don't know
the key to success,
but the key to failure
is trying to please everybody.

Bill Cosby

A honeybee needs both
nectar and pollen to live.
To get these foods,
the honeybee may visit
500 flowers in a single trip.
The insect makes about 15 such trips on a
sunny day,
covering about 3 ½ miles.
A bee must collect nectar
from about
22 million flowers
to make 1 pound of honey.

Melvin and Gilda Berger
*How Do Flies Walk
Upside Down?*

If you are patient
in a moment of anger,
you will spare yourself
one hundred days of tears.

Cambodian proverb

Appear where
they cannot go,
head for where
they least expect you.
To travel hundreds of miles without fatigue,
go over land
where there are no people.

Sun Tzu
The Art of War

The formula for success
is simple:
practice and concentration
then more practice
and more concentration.

Babe Didrikson

Dare he, for whom
circumstances make it possible
to realize his true destiny,
refuse it simply because
he is not prepared
to give up everything else?

Dag Hammarskjold
Markings

Damn the torpedoes!
Full speed ahead!

David G. Farragut
Battle of Mobile Bay
August 5, 1864

Dost thou love life?
Then do not squander time;
for that's the stuff
life is made of.

Benjamin Franklin

Take plenty of time
to make a quick decision.

Bazooka Joe

The sea does not reward
those who are
too anxious, too greedy,
or too impatient.
To dig for treasures shows
not only impatience
and greed,
but lack of faith.
Patience, patience, patience,
is what the sea teaches.
Patience and faith.
One should lie empty, open, choiceless as a
beach—
waiting for
a gift from the sea.

Anne Morrow Lindbergh
Gift From the Sea

I am a great believer in luck,
and I find the harder I work
the more I have of it.

Thomas Jefferson

The man who uses well
what he is given
shall be given more,
and he shall have abundance.
But from the man
who is unfaithful,
even what little
responsibility he has
shall be taken from him.

Jesus
Matthew 25:29

About the Author

Jim Walker is a writer, teacher, and web consult-
ant living in Philadelphia, PA. As a father of four,
he's learned how to move fast!

Please send your comments and favorite quotes
to jimwalker@MindPalace.com

0-595-21044-9